Reel It In
FRESHWATER FISHING

Tina P. Schwartz

PowerKiDS
press.

New York

To Cam—with love, Mom

Published in 2012 by The Rosen Publishing Group, Inc.
29 East 21st Street, New York, NY 10010

First Edition

Editor: Amelie von Zumbusch
Book Design: Kate Laczynski

Photo Credits: Cover © www.iStockphoto.com/George Peters; pp. 4–5 Jupiterimages/Photos.com/Thinkstock; pp. 6, 8, 9 (top, bottom), 10, 16–17, 20, 21 (top) Shutterstock.com; p. 7 (top) © www.iStockphoto.com/Bill Raboin; p. 7 (bottom) © www.iStockphoto.com/Lee Sutterby; pp. 11, 14, 18 iStockphoto/Thinkstock; p. 12 George Grall/Getty Images; p. 13 by Scott Threewitt; p. 15 Fuse/Getty Images; p. 19 Darrin Klimek/Lifesize/Thinkstock; p. 21 (bottom) Hemera/Thinkstock; p. 22 Bob Scott/Photodisc/Thinkstock.

Library of Congress Cataloging-in-Publication Data

Schwartz, Tina P., 1969–
  Freshwater fishing / by Tina P. Schwartz. — 1st ed.
     p. cm.— (Reel it in)
  Includes index.
  ISBN 978-1-4488-6199-6 (library binding) — ISBN 978-1-4488-6357-0 (pbk.)—
ISBN 978-1-4488-6358-7 (6-pack)
  1. Fishing—Juvenile literature. I. Title.
  SH445.S39 2012
  799.1'1—dc23
                                        2011027915

Manufactured in the United States of America

CPSIA Compliance Information: Batch #WW12PK: For Further Information contact Rosen Publishing, New York, New York at 1-800-237-9932

CONTENTS

What Is Freshwater Fishing?

People go freshwater fishing in water that has almost no salt in it. Ponds, lakes, rivers, and streams tend to be freshwater. You can catch freshwater fish in pretty much any water that is not the ocean. Since more Americans live near freshwater than near the ocean, freshwater fishing is the most common kind of fishing in the United States.

You can use **bait**, or things that fish like to eat, to draw fish to you. You can also use **lures**, or pretend fish, instead of bait. The kind of bait or lure that works best depends on what kind of fish you want to catch.

This girl is fishing in a lake. Most of Earth's lakes are freshwater.

Common Freshwater Fish

Almost 60 percent of all fish are saltwater **species**, or kinds. These fish live in or around the ocean. That means that less than half of all fish are freshwater species. A few common types of fish that live in freshwater are bass, trout, catfish, pike, crappies, perch, and walleye.

Tiger muskellunge, such as this one, are members of the pike family. They have one parent that is a northern pike and another that is a muskellunge.

This is a sunfish. Several kinds of sunfish live in North America's lakes, ponds, rivers, and streams.

This salmon has returned to freshwater to have babies. It is swimming up a river.

Landlocked salmon live in freshwater, too. Other salmon are born in freshwater, but **migrate**, or travel, through streams to the ocean when they grow older. After several years, these salmon return to freshwater to have babies. A kind of trout, called a steelhead, makes this migration, too.

Fishing Gear

To fish, you need fishing gear. This is also called **tackle**. Tackle includes many things, such as hooks, lures, bait, rods, and **reels**. Reels hold fishing line. There are several kinds of rods and reels people use when freshwater fishing. One rod is an ultralight fishing rod. This rod works well if you want

As you can see, fishing line passes through loops that hold it against the rod.

to catch small fish. It is shorter, lighter, and bends more than most rods do.

To catch a fish, you need a lure or a hook with bait on it at the end of your line. Swing your rod to **cast** the line. Then wait for a fish to bite.

This trout was caught with a fishing lure. You can see the fish-shaped part of the lure hanging out of the fish's mouth.

Fly-Fishing

It is harder to cast your line in fly-fishing than in other kinds of fishing. If you know someone who is good at fly-fishing, ask that person to show you how to cast your line.

If you want to go fly-fishing, you will need a fly-fishing rod and reel. Fly-fishing is different from other types of fishing because there are special ways to cast your line.

A common way to cast your line in fly-fishing is called the overhead cast. To do this, you look over your shoulder and lift the line backward in a smooth movement, keeping your wrist as straight as possible. Once the line straightens out behind you, you begin the forward cast by bringing your wrist forward. Make sure your line stays above the water so it does not land in a tangled mess.

Different flies are made for catching different kinds of fish. This fly is made for salmon or trout.

Gigging and Noodling

People in the Ozarks often use the gigging method to catch white suckers, such as this one.

Do you know what **gigging** is? It is a type of fishing in which you **spear** your fish. It is a very old form of fishing that was used by Native Americans. Today, gigging is a big sport in the Ozark Mountains in Missouri.

Have you ever gone **noodling**? This is another fishing method that was first used by Native Americans. Noodlers hunt for catfish with their hands instead of a fishing rod. Though noodling can be fun, it can also be unsafe. Some catfish are so large that they can actually pull noodlers down into the water! For that reason, it is illegal in some states.

This man is noodling in Rend Lake in Illinois. Noodlers spend a lot of time in the water, so they need to be strong swimmers.

On the Water

You can go fishing from land or from a boat. Fishing from land can save time and money. However, you may have fewer places to find fish. Without a boat, you will need to stay along a shoreline or in the shallow water of a stream, river, or lake.

Small boats are useful for fishing in a lake, as this family is doing.

If you are fishing from a boat, always wear a life jacket. This is important even if you know how to swim.

Fishing from a boat gives you many places to search for fish. Make sure the boat is in good shape. Have a plan for where you are going. Being aware of the weather and the location of other boats are key to boating safely.

Fishing in Streams and Rivers

FUN FISH FACT

Fish that live in moving water are often very strong from swimming against the current. They tend to be a little smaller than lake fish, though.

Some people walk out into a river to fish. To do this, they often wear *tall* boots *or* waterproof pants with attached boots, called *waders*.

The hardest part of fishing in streams and rivers is that the water is moving. You have to be careful not to lose your footing with the **current**, or moving water, swishing by you!

You will have to decide if you are going to fish where the fish are hiding or where they are eating. Fish like to hide in places that keep them from the current and above-water predators, such as bears or birds. Fish often look for food in places where one stream flows into another. The bends in rivers and streams are also places where fish feed.

Fishing in Ponds and Lakes

This father and son are fishing in a pond. The lily pads nearby suggest that this is a good fishing spot.

A great place for beginning **anglers,** or fishermen, to start fishing is in a lake or a pond. Lakes and ponds have lots of plants for fish to eat and hide under. Logs, rocks, and docks provide places for fish to find shade from the Sun and to hide from bigger fish that want to eat them.

You can fish in a lake or a pond from the shore or from a boat. Look for fish in spots that are deeper or shallower than the areas around them. Look for fish in places where lily pads or underwater plants grow, too.

These girls are fishing in a mountain lake. Some lakes are stocked with fish. This means fish have been added to the lakes so that there will be plenty for anglers to catch.

What to Do with Your Catch

Once you have finally caught a fish, you can have adults clean it and cook it. They can squeeze lemon over it, add some spices, and cook it on a grill! They can even bake it or fry it.

If you do not want to eat your fish, you can use the catch-and-release method of fishing. You remove the hook from the fish's mouth and

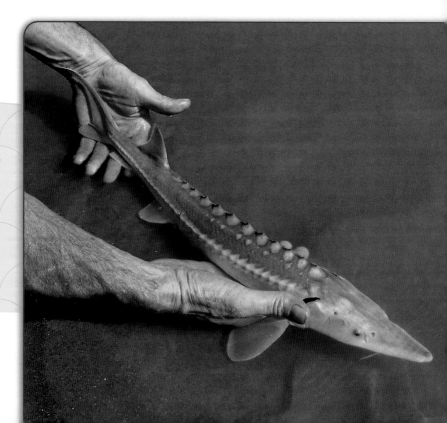

This sturgeon is being released back into the river in which it was caught. Hold a fish gently when you are releasing it.

Many people like to catch and cook fish for dinner when they go on a camping trip. These fish are being cooked in a grill basket over a campfire.

Catching your first fish is exciting! When you catch a fish for the first time, you may want to ask someone to take a picture of you with the fish.

then carefully put the fish back in the water. Be sure to move it back and forth before you let it go. This gets **oxygen** back into its **gills**, so that the fish can breathe.

Knowing Your Surroundings

To be a good angler, be sure to clean up any trash from your fishing trip. Always pick up your extra line as it can easily get tangled around the legs of birds and other animals. Never leave a baited hook anywhere. A bird could eat it by mistake and choke.

This family is fishing in New Jersey's Lake Hopatcong. Do you know of any good freshwater fishing spots near your home?

Lastly, do not be too noisy. If you run around, shout, or play a radio loudly, it will bother those around you, including the fish. Most of all, have fun!

GLOSSARY

anglers (ANG-glerz) People who fish with rods and reels.

bait (BAYT) Something that is used to draw in animals being fished or hunted.

cast (KAST) To throw a fishing line with a rod.

current (KUR-ent) Water that flows in one direction.

gigging (GIG-ing) Catching fish with a sharp thing called a gig or spear.

gills (GILZ) Body parts that fish use for breathing.

landlocked (LAND-lokt) Having to do with water that does not flow into an ocean.

lures (LUHRZ) Fish-shaped objects used for bait.

migrate (MY-grayt) To move from one place to another.

noodling (NOOD-ling) Catching catfish with one's bare hands.

oxygen (OK-sih-jen) A gas that has no color or taste and is necessary for people and animals to breathe.

reels (REELZ) Things around which line or thread is wound.

spear (SPEER) To pierce or jab.

species (SPEE-sheez) One kind of living thing. All people are one species.

tackle (TA-kul) The gear and tools used for a hobby.

23

INDEX

WEB SITES

Due to the changing nature of Internet links, PowerKids Press has developed an online list of Web sites related to the subject of this book. This site is updated regularly. Please use this link to access the list:
www.powerkidslinks.com/reel/fresh/